REAL ESTATE EXAM PREP

100

NEVADA LAW PORTION
REAL ESTATE EXAM QUESTIONS

to help you prepare for your upcoming
state real estate examination

| JOSEPH R. FITZPATRICK |

First Edition

100 NEVADA LAW PORTION REAL ESTATE EXAM QUESTIONS

Authored by Joseph R. Fitzpatrick

First Edition
ISBN: 9781794502598

INTRODUCTION

Thank you for choosing *100 Nevada Law Portion Real Estate Exam Questions* offered by Signature Real Estate School. This study guide contains 100, multiple-choice, practice real estate exam questions to help you pass the Nevada law portion of your state real estate exam.

Testing companies, such as PSI, AMP, and Pearson Vue, hire various test item writers and maintain a bank of hundreds of test questions. Many states will randomly select questions from the bank in order to produce an individual exam thus preventing future test takers from knowing all the answers. Therefore, do not let any real estate school or instructor tell you "this will (or will not) be on your exam."

These 100 questions are *not* the questions from the actual state examination. Although we don't know any specific questions or answers, we do know the content topics and the types of questions that you will likely see.

As you go through the practice questions, you will note that every right-hand page contains the questions while every left-hand page provides answers with explanations for the previous page. You can easily go through a page of questions without being tempted to peek at the answer, nor do you have to keep flipping to an answer key at the back of the book.

Because you will be working these questions without the assistance of a licensed real estate instructor, Signature School of Real Estate designed the answer key so ir not only indicates the correct responses, but also offers detailed explanations.

We hope you find this additional study tool extremely helpful and we wish you the very best of success with your upcoming exam.

1.   B. No license may be issued pursuant to <u>NRS 645.490</u> to a resident of a state other than Nevada until the applicant has appointed in writing the Administrator to be his or her agent, upon whom all process, in any action or proceeding against the applicant, may be served. NRS 645.495.

2.   C. There is nothing wrong with a broker depositing earnest money directly into the firm's trust account.

3.   D. Real estate commissions must be negotiated between the client and the broker. The Real Estate Division certainly has no say or influence on a broker's fee. Commissions are not determined by a group of prominent brokers or that would be collusion and prohibited under anti-trust laws. According to anti-trust laws, there is no "norm."

4.   B. Nevada courts have ruled that net listings are permissible if the seller understands and agrees. They are not advisable as these situations often create a conflict of interest with the seller and the brokerage.

5.   A. Commissioners are appointed by the Governor. NRS 645.050.

6.   The Nevada Real Estate Commission consists of:

    a.   a combination of licensees and members of the public.
    b.   six active real estate licensees and one public member.
    c.   five actively licensed brokers or salespersons.
    d.   five actively licensed brokers or broker-salespersons.

7.   Who may receive compensation from ERRF?

    a.   a cooperating agency which did not receive its share of the commission from the listing firm
    b.   a broker whose commission was refuted by his client
    c.   a seller who pays a commission to a broker under false pretenses
    d.   a buyer who paid a brokerage fee under a brokerage agreement

8.   What is the maximum fine for a violation of Nevada real estate licensing law?

    a. $500 per offense
    b. $5,000 per offense
    c. $10,000 per offense
    d. $20,000 per offense

9.   A salesperson told the buyer that the mold in the laundry room was properly remediated because that is what the sellers told her. Upon inspection, the buyer was informed there were still visible signs of mold as well as mold that was painted over. The salesperson is likely guilty of:

    a.   puffing.
    b.   misrepresentation.
    c.   fraud.
    d.   deceipt.

10.   Broker Bob accepts an earnest money check from his buyers to accompany an offer they wish to present to the foreclosing bank. Having financial troubles, Bob deposits the money in his personal checking account to pay some bills knowing he will be able to replace the funds after his next closing. Which of these is TRUE?

    a.   Bob may do this provided he replaces the funds immediately after the next closing.
    b.   Bob must now wait on presenting the offer as there is now no earnest money.
    c.   Bob can do this as he is the broker.
    d.   Bob cannot do this as this is as it is commingling and conversion.

6.   D. The Commission consists of five actively licensed brokers or broker-salespersons. NRS 645.050, NRS 645.090.

7.   C. ERRF will not settle the non-payment of commissions. The fund is available to consumers who suffered a financial loss as a result of harmful actions by real estate licensees.

8.   C. Presently, a violation could lead to a disciplinary action of a fine of $10,000, plus suspension or revocation of the license.

9.   B. This is misrepresentation as it was innocent in nature. Even though the salesperson was repeating what she had been told by the sellers, it is still incorrect and considered misrepresentation.

10.   D. Even though Bob is the broker, he still cannot legally do this. It is commingling because he deposited the money in his personal checking account. It is also conversion because he spent the money on his bills.

11. Which of these in NOT required for licensure as a Nevada broker?

   a. disclose of any past felony convictions or real estate license suspensions or revocations
   b. provide the business location and any fictitious names to be used
   c. submit a 3-year work history
   d. produce a statement of previous real estate experience, if any

12. The seller's broker knows the home has termites and that the husband was murdered in the house. The broker must disclose to the buyer:

   a. the murder but not the termites.
   b. the termites but not the murder.
   c. neither fact.
   d. both facts.

13. When a Nevada broker represents both parties in the same transaction, the broker shall obtain the written consent of all parties. That written consent must:

   a. include a statement that the licensee has a conflict of interest.
   b. contain a description of the transaction.
   c. state that the licensee is representing multiple parties with adverse interests.
   d. All of the above

14. The listing salesperson is showing his listing to very interested buyers. The asking price is $249,000. The salesperson suggests to the buyers that they make an offer of $230,000 because the salesperson believes that might be accepted by his sellers. Has the salesperson violated the licensing law?

   a. No, because he is representing the buyers whenever he writes an offer on their behalf.
   b. No, because the salesperson is attempting to generate some sort of purchasing activity on the property.
   c. Yes, because he offered the property at a price not authorized by the sellers and is breaching his fiduciary duty.
   d. Yes, because the offer is not a bona fide offer.

15. A salesperson procures a ready, willing, and able buyer for her seller. The seller accepts the offer and then gets cold feet the next day and withdraws his acceptance. The salesperson:

   a. may sue the seller.
   b. cannot collect a commission as the transaction will not close.
   c. might still be entitled to collect a commission.
   d. may retain the earnest money deposit in lieu of a commission.

11.   C. A person may not be licensed as a real estate broker unless the person has been actively engaged as a full-time licensed real estate broker-salesperson or salesperson in this State, or actively engaged as a full-time licensed real estate broker, broker-salesperson or salesperson in another state or the District of Columbia, for at least 2 of the 4 years immediately preceding the issuance of a broker's license. This is a more stringent requirement than just a 3-year work history. NRS 645.330.

12.   B. Circumstances associated with "stigmatized" properties, such as a murder, are not considered to be material facts in Nevada as well as most other states. The presence of termites is a material fact and must be disclosed.

13.   D. These requirements are included in the *Consent to Act* form. NRS 645.252.

14.   C. The listing agent's suggestion to the buyer or the buyer's agent of a price the seller would be willing to accept other than the list price is prohibited (unless the seller has given authorization for the listing agent to do so). NRS 645.635.

15.   C. A broker has earned a commission upon producing a ready, willing, and able buyer. Even though the transaction will not close, the firm may still be entitled to a commission as they procured such a buyer. The salesperson cannot sue the seller for commission, only the broker may. The firm has no rights to the earnest money, and the buyer did nothing wrong.

16. Can a Nevada licensee fulfill all continuing education requirements online?

    a. No, Nevada does not permit continuing education online.
    b. No, at least 50% of the continuing education requirement must be taken in a live, classroom environment.
    c. Yes, provided the courses include 3 hours of agency, 3 hours of law or legal update, 3 hours of contracts, and 3 hours of ethics.
    d. Yes, as long as all of the school's online courses have been approved by the Commission.

17. Which of these agency relationships is NOT permissible in Nevada?

    a. single agency
    b. assigned agency
    c. multiple representation
    d. transaction brokerage

18. A person who violates any provisions of NRS 645 is guilty of a:

    a. gross misdemeanor.
    b. felony.
    c. tort.
    d. crime of moral turpitude.

19. An accounting of an advanced fee must be provided to the principal within how many days of collecting the money?

    a. 30
    b. 60
    c. 90
    d. 180

20. The listing agent decides he and his wife would like to purchase the property themselves. As a Nevada licensee, the listing agent:

    a. cannot purchase his own listing as it is a conflict of interest.
    b. must be a buyer's agent only and have his broker re-assign the listing and arrange for seller representation.
    c. must be a dual agent.
    d. must maintain his duties as the sellers' agent.

16.   B. At least 50% of the continuing education requirement must be taken in a live, classroom environment.

17.   D. Transaction brokerage is not recognized in Nevada. NRS 645.252, NRS 645.253.

18.   A. A person who violates any other provision of this chapter, if a natural person, is guilty of a gross misdemeanor, (and if a limited-liability company, partnership, association or corporation, shall be punished by a fine of not more than $2,500.)

19.   C. The requirement is 90 days. NRS 645.322

20.   B. The licensee can certainly purchase his own listing, but he would then be looking out for his own best interests instead of the seller's. It is therefore not possible for him to represent the seller in any way, thus eliminating dual agency or seller agency.

21. A Nevada licensee must provide the seller's *Seller's Real Property Disclosure* for all of the following properties EXCEPT a(n):

    a.   new home.
    b.   For Sale by Owner.
    c.   resale property.
    d.   fourplex.

22. The *Duties Owed by a Nevada Licensee* form must be supplied to prospective purchasers or tenants:

    a.   at an open house.
    b.   before they are shown any properties.
    c.   no later than the time of entering an agreement to purchase or lease.
    d.   at the close of escrow.

23. Regarding the duty of confidentiality, Nevada law requires that the:

    a.   broker maintain all information as confidential for a period of two years.
    b.   broker keep all information confidential that the seller has provided about the property.
    c.   broker disclose information that materially affects the property even when the buyer does not ask for it.
    d.   broker disclose everything that the seller shares.

24. Charles, a Nevada licensee, tells the lender that the sales price on a property is $250,000, when in fact, it is $220,000. The:

    a.   licensee has done nothing wrong as long as the appraisal substantiates the price.
    b.   buyer is likely to receive an interest rate discount.
    c.   buyer can receive a lower mortgage payment.
    d.   licensee can have his or her license suspended or revoked.

25. An agent orders a home warranty for her buyers knowing she will receive a $50 referral fee from the home warranty company. Is this a violation of the Nevada license law?

    a.   No, because the referral fee is less than the $100 limit.
    b.   No, because referral fees from other real estate professionals are not a violation of the Nevada license law.
    c.   Yes, because a salesperson may not receive compensation from anyone other than her employing broker.
    d.   Yes, because only the seller may compensate a salesperson.

21.   A. An SRPD is not required on a new home sale. NRS 113.130/SRPD form.

22.   C. This is difficult to find in 645, but the Division's Informational Bulletin #005 says, "It should still be signed as soon as practicable but in no event later than the time of a written contract." A written contract would include any brokerage agreement including listing agreements, buyer brokerage agreements, property management agreements as well as any purchase agreements or lease agreements.

23.   C. The broker, or the licensee acting on behalf of the broker, must disclose information that materially affects the property even when the buyer does not ask for it. These facts must be disclosed even if it negatively affects the seller or the future of the transaction. The duty of confidentiality lasts for one year.

24.   D. NRS 645.635 states that the Commission can discipline a licensee for "Representing to any lender, guaranteeing agency or any other interested party, verbally or through the preparation of false documents, an amount in excess of the actual sale price of the real estate or terms differing from those actually agreed upon."

25.   C. A broker could receive a referral fee from the home warranty company if it is disclosed to all parties A salesperson or broker-salesperson may only be compensated by the employing broker. There is no such thing as a $100 limit. NRS 645.633.

26.   All of the following are grounds for disciplinary action EXCEPT a licensee:

a.   giving information on a rental to a tenant without the landlord's permission.
b.   trying to negotiate a sale of property directly with an owner while that owner is currently exclusively listed with another broker.
c.   refusing to show property to a prospective purchaser due to poor credit.
d.   refusing to write a low offer that the licensee knows will not be accepted.

27.   Nevada recognizes three types of agency relationships. They are:

a.   subagency, dual agency, seller agency
b.   single agency, multiple representation, and assigned agency
c.   seller agency, buyer agency, transactional brokerage
d.   fiduciary agency, universal agency, multiple agency

28.   In Nevada, may a broker legally collect a commission from both the seller and the buyer?

a.   Yes, if the broker is a transaction broker.
b.   Yes, if the broker discloses it.
c.   Yes, if both parties give their informed, written consent.
d.   No.

29.   Bob, a Nevada real estate salesperson, puts his own home on the market and places a sign in the yard. Bob's sign must:

a.   identify the brokerage name and Bob's name.
b.   Include the word "REALTOR®."
c.   indicate his name and contact information.
d.   identify the brokerage name.

30.   All funds received by the broker on behalf of the principal must be deposited in the trust account or escrow opened:

a.   within three days of receiving the offer.
b.   within 10 business days of execution of the contract.
c.   within five calendar days of receiving the offer.
d.   within one banking day of acceptance of the offer.

26.   C. Refusing to show property because of the client's credit status is not illegal and in fact, is good business practice. The other acts are prohibited under NRS 645.630-635.

27.   B. NRS 645.252 and NRS 645.254

28.   C. If the licensee receives compensation from more than one party in a real estate transaction, full disclosure to *and* consent from each party to the real estate transaction is required. Simply disclosing it is not enough. NAC 645.605.

29.   D. The name of a brokerage firm under which a real estate broker does business or with which a real estate broker-salesperson or salesperson is associated must be clearly identified with prominence in any advertisement Including signs). NAC 645.610.

30.   D. If a real estate broker receives money which belongs to others, the real estate broker shall promptly deposit the money in a separate checking account located in a bank or credit union in this state which must be designated a trust account. NRS 645.310. "Promptly" is considered to be one business day.

31. When writing an offer, a salesperson received an earnest money deposit from her buyers, made payable to the brokerage. According to Nevada law, the salesperson must:

    a.   give it to the seller upon presentation of the offer.
    b.   deposit the money in her trust account immediately.
    c.   deposit the funds in a separate trust account solely for that transaction.
    d.   turn the funds over to her broker promptly.

32. A salesperson engaged in several activities that resulted in the salesperson appearing before the Commission. What is the impact of the salesperson's behavior on the broker when the violations are brought before the Commission?

    a.   She will be disciplined and have her license revoked.
    b.   She must surrender her license.
    c.   She may be disciplined for failure to supervise.
    d.   She is liable for the salesperson's actions, but the salesperson is not liable.

33. Several weeks after the close of escrow, a broker-salesperson received a nice thank you note with a bonus check from the seller. The broker-salesperson cashed the check and kept the funds for her own use. Which of the following is TRUE?

    a.   This is a violation of Nevada regulations and the broker-salesperson may be disciplined.
    b.   This is perfectly legitimate, but only if the check were payable to the broker-salesperson.
    c.   This is acceptable provided the broker is aware.
    d.   This is legal as long as the bonus check is not in excess of $500.

34. Nevada real estate brokers are required to keep transaction records for:

    a.   one year.
    b.   five years from last activity.
    c.   forever.
    d.   None of the above

35. Nevada real estate license applicants must be at least what age?

    a.   17
    b.   18
    c.   21
    d.   There is no age requirement.

31.   D. Every real estate salesperson or broker-salesperson who receives any money on behalf of a broker or owner-developer shall pay over the money promptly to the real estate broker or owner-developer. NRS 645.310.

32.   C. It is not a guaranteed suspension, revocation, or surrender of the broker's license – that will be determined by the Commission. She *may* be disciplined for failure to supervise.

33.   A. A salesperson or broker-salesperson may only receive compensation from the employing broker. NRS 645.280.

34.   B. The broker must keep the transaction files for 5 years from the last activity and those files must be kept at a location approved by the Real Estate Division. NAC 645.650.

35.   B. NAC 645.100 indicates an applicant must be at least 18 years of age.

36.   In Nevada, the person or agency charged with investigating transaction files and trust records of brokers and owner-developers is the:

   a.   Division interloper.
   b.   Administrator of the Division.
   c.   Nevada Real Estate Commission.
   d.   Attorney General.

37.   While taking his pre-licensing course, Oliver sells his neighbor's house who agreed to pay Oliver a 6% commission. After closing, the neighbor refused to pay the commission. Can Oliver sue to recover payment?

   a.   Yes. Oliver performed as hired.
   b.   Yes, but the broker must sue for commissions.
   c.   No. One must be licensed to earn a commission.
   d.   None of the above

38.   Which of the following is NOT a violation of Nevada licensing laws?

   a.   acting as a principal in a transaction
   b.   a fraudulent action in real estate sales prior to his licensing in Nevada
   c.   advertising oneself as a "REALTOR®" without belonging to the Association of REALTORS®
   d.   guaranteeing future profits to a buyer when the buyer resells

39.   The maximum amount an individual may claim from the recovery fund pertaining to any one transaction is actual damages but no more than:

   a. $25,000.
   b. $50,000.
   c. $100,000.
   d. $300,000.

40.   Which element, if missing in an exclusive right to sell listing agreement, could result in a suspension, revocation, or fine?

   a.   exact expiration date
   b.   automatic renewal clause
   c.   salesperson's name
   d.   broker protection clause

36.   B. This is the responsibility of the Administrator as an agent for the Division. NRS 645.195.

37.   C. One has to be licensed in order to perform real estate services for compensation. It is true that only the broker can sue for commissions, but even if the broker sues, the broker will lose as Oliver was not licensed.

38.   A. The licensee can act as a principal provided he or she discloses the license status. All of the other choices are prohibited under NRS 645.630-635.

39.   A. "When any person obtains a final judgment in any court of competent jurisdiction against any licensee or licensees pursuant to this chapter, upon grounds of fraud, misrepresentation or deceit with reference to any transaction for which a license is required pursuant to this chapter, that person, upon termination of all proceedings, including appeals in connection with any judgment, may file a verified petition in the court in which the judgment was entered for an order directing payment out of the Fund in the amount of the unpaid actual damages included in the judgment, but not more than $25,000 per judgment."

40.   A. Every exclusive agency representation agreement is required to be in writing and have a clearly defined expiration date. NRS 645.320.

41. The sellers listed their townhouse for six months, but after two months they notified the broker they no longer wanted to sell the property. Which of the following statements is TRUE?

    a.   They terminated the listing agreement and there are no further obligations.
    b.   They have withdrawn the broker's right to sell and may be liable to the broker.
    c.   They are required to leave the home on the market.
    d.   The sellers are liable for a commission if the broker sells the property after the withdrawal of the listing.

42. A Nevada licensee's first license term is for a period of:

    a.   6 months.
    b.   one year.
    c.   two years.
    d.   four years.

43. All of the following Nevada contracts must be in writing EXCEPT a(n):

    a.   exclusive agency listing.
    b.   open listing.
    c.   exclusive right to sell listing.
    d.   real estate sales contract.

44. A salesperson must submit all paperwork on a new transaction to the broker within what number of days?

    a.   1 business day
    b.   3 calendar days
    c.   5 calendar days
    d.   10 days

45. All of the following are requirements of a property manager permit holder EXCEPT:

    a.   24 hours of pre-permit education.
    b.   3 hours of continuing education in property management.
    c.   a real estate license.
    d.   a broker's license.

41.   B. The sellers have withdrawn the broker's right to sell and may be liable to the broker. The sellers could be liable to the broker for expenses or a commission if the property is sold at a later date – the terms of the withdrawal would dictate the seller's potential liability for such. They do not have to keep the property on the market.

42.   B. In July of 2015, the Commission changed license terms back to the way they were historically which is one year for an initial license and two years for subsequent licenses. NRS 645.490

43.   B. Open listings may be oral or in writing. Exclusive agency agreements must be in writing per NRS 645.320.   Real estate contracts must also be in writing per Nevada law.

44.   C. NAC 645.650

45.   D. A property manager does not have to be a broker. The educational requirement for the property management permit is 24 hours. There is a 3-hour continuing education course requirement in property management. A property management permit can be issued to a qualified salesperson, broker-salesperson, or broker. NRS 645.6052.

46.   Who MUST have a real estate license?

    a.   a bankruptcy trustee
    b.   a property manager
    c.   the owner of the property being sold or leased
    d.   an executor of an estate

47.   A Nevada licensee had his out-of-state license revoked for commingling and conversion. The licensee:

    a.   will not be disciplined in Nevada.
    b.   will automatically lose his Nevada license.
    c.   may have his Nevada license suspended or revoked.
    d.   does not have to disclose the out-of-state incident to the Nevada Real Estate Division.

48.   Which of the following may have an active Nevada real estate license?

    a.   suspended licensee
    b.   nonresident of Nevada
    c.   depository financial institution
    d.   Division employee

49.   In Nevada, a partnership, association, or corporation will be granted a Nevada real estate license only if:

    a.   every member actively participating in the brokerage business has a broker's license.
    b.   there is a member who meets the qualifications of a broker.
    c.   all papers are filed with the Secretary of State
    d.   All of the above

50.   An unlicensed assistant may perform all of the following activities EXCEPT:

    a.   prepare mailings and promotional materials.
    b.   assemble disclosure documents required for a closing.
    c.   compute commission checks.
    d.   explain simple contract documents to prospective purchasers.

46.   B. A property manager must hold a real estate license. The other three choices are exemptions under NRS 645.240.

47.   C. "The Commission may take action pursuant to NRS 645.630 against a person who is subject to that section for the suspension or revocation of a real estate broker's, broker-salesperson's or salesperson's license issued by any other jurisdiction."

48.   B. Non-residents of Nevada may have an active license provided they meet Commission prescribed requirements. A Division employee is prohibited from having an active license (NRS 6435.130). A suspended licensee's license will be on inactive status, not active. A depository financial institution is also prohibited from having a license (NRS 645.335).

49.   B. In Nevada, a partnership, association, or corporation will be granted a Nevada real estate license only if there is a member who meets the qualifications of a broker. NRS 645.370.

50.   D. Explaining documents and contracts to clients is an act which requires a license. The other activities are acceptable for an unlicensed assistant to perform.

51.   A broker's price opinion in Nevada must include:

    a.   the name of the real estate broker.
    b.   a statement as to the purpose of the opinion.
    c.   a statement that it is an opinion of value and is not an appraisal.
    d.   All of the above

52.   The parties to a multiple representation transaction can provide their informed, written consent by executing what document?

    a.   Duties Owed
    b.   SRPD
    c.   Cons
    d.   Resi

53.   A sale___ the agent's accomplishments, production awards, market share, w___ information. The salesperson must also include in the ad:

    a.   her real estate license number.
    b.   the registered name of her brokerage firm.
    c.   the wording, "This ad approved by the Nevada Real Estate Division."
    d.   All of the above

54.   The Real Estate Division has made available a booklet that contains all the disclosures that must be made per federal, state, and local laws and regulations regarding a residential transaction. This booklet is called:

    a.   *Seller's Real Property Disclosure*
    b.   *Real Property Disclosure Guide*
    c.   *Residential Disclosure Guide*
    d.   *Did You Know?*

55.   Which of the following omissions from an agent's web site could result in a fine from the Nevada Real Estate Division?

    a.   contact information
    b.   the brokerage name
    c.   pictures of the properties
    d.   None of the above

51.   D. A broker's price opinion must contain all 3 items and more. NRS 645.2515.

52.   C. The *Consent to Act* is utilized so the parties to the transaction can acknowledge and agree to a multiple representation transaction. NRS 645.253.

53.   B. The name of a brokerage firm under which a real estate broker does business or with which a real estate broker-salesperson or salesperson is associated must be clearly identified with prominence in any advertisement. NAC 645.610.

54.   C. The booklet is called the *Residential Disclosure Guide*. NRS 645.194.

55.   B. A web site is treated like any other advertisement, and the name of the brokerage firm must be clearly identified with prominence. NAC 645.610.

56.   In Las Vegas, the standard real estate commission rate is:

    a.   5%
    b.   6%
    c.   7%
    d.   None of the above

57.   An earnest money deposit:

    a.   is legally required with an offer.
    b.   may not be in the form of cash.
    c.   can be anything of value that is acceptable to the offeree.
    d.   in the form of promissory note is illegal in Nevada.

58.   Must a Nevada broker maintain a trust account?

    a.   No, but only if the Division has exempted the broker from maintaining one.
    b.   No.
    c.   Yes.
    d.   Yes, and the account information must be on file with the Commission.

59.   A new Nevada broker opening a brokerage firm will handle earnest money. Which statement is FALSE?

    a.   She must notify the Division of the banks where she has trust accounts.
    b.   She may have several trust accounts.
    c.   She is the trustee of the trust account.
    d.   The Real Estate Division cannot inspect her trust account records without a complaint from a consumer first.

60.   A broker-salesperson leaves the field for expiration date of his listing agreement with the seller blank. Which of these statements is TRUE?

    a.   He has violated a Nevada statute as every listing must have a specific termination date.
    b.   He could be disciplined by the Nevada Real Estate Commission.
    c.   He could be fined as much as $10,000 and have his license suspended or revoked.
    d.   All of the above

56.   D. Per anti-trust laws, there is no standard brokerage fee. To suggest there is, is a violation.

57.   C. Earnest money deposits in the form of cash or promissory note are legal. An earnest money deposit is not legally required, but is common. The earnest money deposit can be anything of value that is acceptable to the offeree. NRS 645.630.

58.   B. NAC 645.175. A Nevada broker is not required to maintain a trust account provided he is not performing property management services and turns all deposits over to escrow.

59.   D. The Real Estate Division can inspect a broker's transaction of trust account records at any time, even without a complaint from a consumer.

60.   D. All statements are true. NRS 645.633.

61.   A Nevada licensee may lawfully collect a commission from:

    a.   the cooperating broker.
    b.   either the buyer or the seller.
    c.   the employing broker.
    d.   All of the above

62.   A Nevada broker is opening a branch office in Reno. The broker appoints salesperson, Wanda, as the branch manager. Which of the following statements is TRUE?

    a.   Only the broker can be the branch manager for the Reno office.
    b.   Wanda must be a Reno resident.
    c.   The broker will be granted a branch office license as he has named a branch manager.
    d.   The broker's application will be denied.

63.   Beyond the initial licensing period, a Nevada real estate license expires every:

    a.   48 months.
    b.   24 months.
    c.   30 months.
    d.   15 months.

64.   A listing broker wishes to sue her seller for a commission. She must demonstrate all of the following EXCEPT:

    a.   she was properly licensed at the time she performed.
    b.   there was a brokerage agreement in effect.
    c.   the property successfully closed escrow.
    d.   she procured a ready, willing, and able purchaser who met price and terms acceptable to the seller.

65.   The top brokers in Las Vegas meet to share ideas on increasing profits. Which of the following can the brokers agree to do?

    a.   charge only an 8% commission rate
    b.   refuse to cooperate with discount brokerage firms
    c.   divide the city into geographic areas and agree that each broker will confine his business to his area
    d.   None of the above

61.   C. A Nevada licensee can only collect a commission from the employing broker. NRS 645.633.

62.   D. The application for the branch office will be denied because the broker is appointing a salesperson to be the branch manager. A branch manager must be a broker or a broker-salesperson who, within the preceding 4 years, has had 2 years of active experience. NAC 645.177.

63.   B. The initial license period for an original license as a real estate broker, broker-salesperson or salesperson is a period of 12 consecutive months beginning on the first day of the first calendar month after the original license is issued by the Division. Thereafter, each subsequent license period is a period of 24 consecutive months beginning on the first day of the first calendar month after a renewal of the license is issued by the Division for the subsequent license period. NRS 645.780 references the former rules. The Division changed this effective July 2015.

64.   C. The transaction need not close escrow for the broker to be entitled. A broker is said to have earned a commission when that broker procures a ready, willing, and able buyer to meet the price and terms acceptable to the seller. That broker must be actively licensed at the time of procurement and authorized for the payment of a commission under a brokerage agreement.

65.   D. All of the choices are in violation of anti-trust laws. Market allocation, price fixing (commission setting), and boycotting are specific violations.

66. When must a *Seller's Real Property Disclosure* form be delivered to the buyer?

    a.   no later than ten days before the property is conveyed to the purchaser
    b.   at the time that the seller agrees to the offer
    c.   at the time of the home inspection
    d.   at the time of closing

67. If any, one associate makes a misrepresentation to a client, the broker:

    a.   cannot be disciplined because he would have no way to know of the misrepresentation.
    b.   should have offered better training and management.
    c.   may be disciplined for failure to supervise.
    d.   will have his license suspended until a monetary fine is paid.

68. All of these require disclosure to the Nevada Real Estate Division within 10 days of their occurrence EXCEPT:

    a.   a name change of the brokerage.
    b.   a change of address for the brokerage.
    c.   the broker's completion of continuing education courses.
    d.   the termination of a licensee.

69. Which of the following continuing education courses is NOT required for a broker-salesperson to renew his license:

    a.   property management
    b.   broker management
    c.   agency relationships
    d.   law and ethics

70. Steve Harvey, Ellen Degeneres, and Montel Williams have formed a real estate team working for broker Brad Pitt at Ocean's Realty, Inc. Which of the following is permissible pertaining to advertising by the team?

    a.   The team advertises as "The Ocean Team."
    b.   The team advertises as "The Harvey Team."
    c.   The team advertises as "Montel's Superstars."
    d.   None of the above

66.   A. The disclosure must be delivered to the buyers no later than 10 days before the property is conveyed to the purchaser (close of escrow) NRS 113.

67.   C. The broker can be disciplined for failure to supervise. Even if the broker had no knowledge of the misrepresentation, he is still responsible for the actions of his licensee. Perhaps the broker should have offered better training and management, but we do not know if it was lacking or not. We do not know if his license will be suspended or not.

68.   C. There is no need to notify the Division of the completion of a continuing education course until it is time to submit C.E. certificates.

69.   A. A property management continuing education course *could* be taken by a broker-salesperson for credit, but it is not required unless the licensee is a property management permit holder.

70.   B. Advertising must contain the last name of one of the team members. NAC 645.611.

71.   The resale package documents from a Common Interest Community are:

    a.   due by the close of escrow.
    b.   always paid for by the buyer.
    c.   only required on new construction.
    d.   required to be provided by the seller at the seller's expense

72.   Declaring a designated agency eliminates the need for what Nevada form?

    a.   Consent to Act
    b.   Duties Owed
    c.   SRPD
    d.   None of the above

73.   A new agent is looking for listings, and in an attempt to get a quick listing, he door knocks and tells the homeowners that a particular ethnic group is buying all the homes in the neighborhood. The agent is:

    a.   "blockbusting."
    b.   creating "panic selling."
    c.   subject to a fine and have his license suspended or revoked.
    d.   All of the above

74.   An exclusive-right-to-sell listing must contain all of the following EXCEPT:

    a.   list price.
    b.   the seller's and broker's signatures.
    c.   a fixed termination date.
    d.   an automatic renewal clause.

75.   James wants to obtain his broker-salesperson's license. Which of these is NOT a requirement for him to satisfy?

    a.   show proof of 64 college credits
    b.   show proof of 2 years of real estate licensing experience
    c.   disclose any prior convictions of a felony
    d.   demonstrate he is of good character

71.   D. The law states that the seller has the obligation to provide and pay for the documents. The CIC docs are applicable in any transaction where an HOA exists. The contract dictates when the docs must be delivered to the buyer for review, and it is certainly before the close of escrow.

72.   A. The Consent to Act is not needed in a designated agency as there is no dual agency/multiple representation relationship. NRS 645.253

73.   D. These acts are prohibited under the federal Fair Housing Act. The licensee's activities would likely be treated as "any other conduct which constitutes deceitful, fraudulent or dishonest dealing" and therefore punishable under NRS 645.633.

74.   D. The listing *cannot* have an automatic renewal clause.

75.   B. Surprisingly, experience is not required for a broker-salesperson's license.

76.   An applicant for an initial Nevada salesperson's license must complete:

a.   24 classroom hours of Nevada law.
b.   64 semester units of college coursework.
c.   a 90-hour approved pre-licensing course.
d.   a property management course.

77.   Waiver of pre-licensing educational requirements for brokers and broker-salespersons is made for active, full-time experience as follows:

a.   15 credits for every two years.
b.   16 credits for every two years.
c.   8 credits for every one year.
d.   There is no waiver for experience.

78.   Are there any situations where the *Duties Owed by a Nevada Licensee* does not apply?

a.   A *Duties Owed* is not required on a sale where a licensee represents both the seller and the buyer because a *Consent to Act* will be utilized.
b.   A *Duties Owed* is not required on a sale where a licensee represents either the seller or the buyer, and the other party is unrepresented.
c.   A *Duties Owed* is not required on the sale of corporeal personalty.
d.   A *Duties Owed* is not required where a licensee is acting as a principal in the transaction.

79.   The parties to a transaction must be provided with a closing statement by the broker:

a.   at closing.
b.   within one business day before close of escrow
c.   within 10 business days after close of escrow
d.   never

80.   A seller refuses to show his house for rent to any members of German descent. Upon being refused an opportunity to preview the house because of their national origin, the tenants file a complaint with the Nevada Real Estate Division. Upon confirmation of the discrimination, the Division will:

a.   assist the tenants with legal action.
b.   begin a formal investigation.
c.   issue an injunction.
d.   do nothing, as the Division has no jurisdiction.

76.   C. NAC 645.435.

77.   B. Each person who holds a license as a real estate broker, broker-salesperson or salesperson, or an equivalent license, issued by a state or territory of the United States, or the District of Columbia, is entitled to receive credit for the equivalent of 16 semester units of college level courses for each 2 years of active experience that, during the immediately preceding 10 years, the person has obtained while he or she has held such a license, not to exceed 8 years of active experience.

78.   C. "Corporeal personalty" is fancy language for tangible, personal property such as a washer and dryer. This is not the sale of real property so there is no "*Duties Owed*" form required. The other transactions require the form.

79.   C. The requirement is within 10 business days after the closing although the title company's (escrow holder) delivery of a closing statement fulfills this broker requirement. NRS 645.635.

80.   D. The Real Estate Division will not get involved as this is a private transaction not involving a real estate licensee. The Division has no jurisdiction.

81.   The listing agent delivered the seller's SRPD to the buyer's agent which did not disclose the property recently had mold remediation. Although the listing agent had no knowledge of the problem, he was sued along with the seller by the buyer upon discovery of the issue. Will the listing agent likely be found liable for the seller's concealment?

    a.   No, because he is not liable for his client's misrepresentation if he had no knowledge of the matter.
    b.   No, because he is not expected to be a mold expert.
    c.   Yes, because he should have known through the exercise of due diligence.
    d.   Yes, because he is responsible to verify the information conveyed in the SRPD.

82.   Jones has resigned from Wayside Realty and her license has been returned to the Division. How much time does she have to affiliate with another broker before her license is inactivated?

    a.   5 days
    b.   10 days
    c.   30 days
    d.   None of the above

83.   A Nevada licensee applicant from another state may not be required to take or pass the national portion of the state exam provided:

    a.   the applicant holds an *active* license in the other state.
    b.   the other state's educational requirements are comparable to those of Nevada.
    c.   the applicant's license is in good standing with that state's licensing authority.
    d.   All of the above

84.   Unless extended for further investigation, the Division has how long to act on an applicant's application for licensure?

    a.   30 days
    b.   45 days
    c.   60 days
    d.   90 days

85.   In order for a brokerage firm to conduct property management services:

    a.   The broker must appoint a broker or broker-salesperson as the designated property manager with the Division.
    b.   The designated property manager must have both an active real estate license and a property management permit.
    c.   The designated property manager must have at least two out of the last four years of active experience.
    d.   All of the above

81.   A. A licensee may not be held liable for a misrepresentation made by his or her client unless the licensee knew the client made the misrepresentation and failed to inform the person to whom the client made the misrepresentation that the statement was false. NRS 645.259

82.   B. The deadline (like many other Division deadlines) is 10 days.

83.   D. NRS 645.332.

84.   C. 60 days. NRS 645.420.

85.   D. NRS 645.6055.

86.   Which of the following statements is TRUE regarding the hearing process pertaining to a licensee facing a disciplinary action?

   a.   The hearing must be scheduled within 60 days of the filing of the complaint by the Administrator.
   b.   The Commission must send written notice of its final decision to the licensee within 30 days after the hearing.
   c.   If the decision of the Commission is in favor of the licensee, the decision is final.
   d.   If the license is revoked, no license will be issued to the licensee within 10 years of the date of revocation.

87.   A Nevada licensee forgot to renew her Nevada real estate license before the license expiration date. Which of the following statements is TRUE?

   a.   She may renew her license if she completes additional education requirements.
   b.   She may renew her license within one year if she pays additional fees.
   c.   She must reapply for a license as an original, first-time applicant.
   d.   She may only renew her license with both the completion of additional education and the payment of additional fees.

88.   Which of the following statements is TRUE regarding a business broker's permit?

   a.   An applicant for an original permit must demonstrate the completion of a 24-hour approved course in business brokerage.
   b.   The renewal of the permit must include a 3-hour approved course in business brokerage.
   c.   The expiration date of the permit coincides with the expiration date of the licensee's real estate license.
   d.   All of the above

89.   When must the *Seller's Real Property Disclosure* statement be provided to the buyers?

   a.   as soon as practical, but no later than the signing of the sales contract
   b.   within 4 working days of closing
   c.   at least 10 days before the property is conveyed to the purchaser
   d.   during the due diligence period

90.   The Nevada *Duties Owed* form?

   a.   lists the broker's responsibilities to the client.
   b.   creates a contract for services.
   c.   forms an agency relationship.
   d.   obligates the signor for compensation.

86.   C. The hearing must be scheduled within 90 days of the filing of the complaint by the Administrator, not 60. The Commission must send written notice of its final decision to the licensee within 60 days after the hearing, not 30. If the license is revoked, no license will be issued to the licensee within 1 year of the date of revocation, not 10. NRS 645.680-770.

87.   B. She may renew her license within one year of the expiration date if she pays additional fees. NRS 645.785.

88.   D. NRS 645.863.

89.   C. The disclosure must be delivered to the buyers no later than 10 days before the property is conveyed to the purchaser (close of escrow) NRS 113.

90.   A. NAC 645.175-178.

91.   A Nevada licensee may prepare a broker's price opinion for a fee provided:

   a. it contains a statement that clarifies the opinion is not an appraisal.
   b. the broker is ultimately responsible for supervising the licensee's preparation of the report.
   c. the licensee discloses any existing or contemplated interest in the property.
   d. All of the above

92.   During a Nevada licensee's first license year:

   a.   an approved, 45-hour post licensing course must be completed.
   b.   an approved, post licensing course must be completed either online or in a classroom setting.
   c.   pre-licensing hours can count toward the post licensing requirement.
   d.   the post licensing requirement may be waived if the licensee holds a license in another state.

93.   Jose is completing his continuing education requirements. Which of these statements is TRUE?

   a.   He must submit a minimum of six hours in personal development courses.
   b.   He must show a minimum of six hours of agency and six hours of Nevada law.
   c.   If Jose is a broker-salesperson, he must also show six hours in broker management.
   d.   He must submit 24 hours of approved continuing education courses every two years.

94.   The Real Estate Division has made available a booklet that contains all the disclosures that must be made per federal, state, and local laws and regulations regarding a residential transaction. This booklet is called:

   a.   *Seller's Real Property Disclosure*
   b.   *Real Property Disclosure Guide*
   c.   *Residential Disclosure Guide*
   d.   *Did You Know?*

95.   A Nevada salesperson's first license was issued on November 3, 2019. When will his license expire?

   a.   November 30, 2020
   b.   November 30, 2021
   c.   November 3, 2020
   d.   December 30, 2021

91.   D. All of the statements are true. NRS 645.2515

92.   D. It is a 30-hour requirement, not 45. The course must be a live course, not online. Pre-licensing hours do not count toward the post-licensing requirement. The requirement for post licensing may be waived for a licensee who holds a real estate license issued by another state. NAC 645.4442.

93.   D. Jose must submit 24 hours of approved continuing education courses every two years. No more than three hours in personal development courses, a minimum of three hours of agency, and a minimum of three hours of Nevada law. If a broker-salesperson, Jose must also show at least three hours in broker management.

94.   C. The booklet is called the *Residential Disclosure Guide*. NRS 645.194.

95.   A. It expires the last day of the month, 1 year later. NRS 645.780.

96.   The seller's agent is required to disclose to potential buyers:

    a.   there was a death in the home.
    b.   the home was occupied by a person with AIDS.
    c.   there are spirits haunting the house.
    d.   the hot water heater is not working.

97.   When a licensee obtains a signed brokerage agreement from the client, the licensee shall deliver a copy of that agreement to the client:

    a.   immediately.
    b.   immediately upon signing or a reasonable time thereafter.
    c.   within 5 business days.
    d.   within 10 days.

98.   The obligation of confidentiality in Nevada lasts:

    a.   forever.
    b.   for six months after closing.
    c.   for 1 year after termination of the agency.
    d.   There is no obligation of confidentiality in Nevada.

99.   Which of these is responsible for adopting Nevada real estate regulations?

    a.   the Division
    b.   the Nevada Real Estate Commission
    c.   the Attorney General
    d.   the Administrator

100.   Which of these licenses require two years of prior licensing history?

    a.   time share agent
    b.   salesperson
    c.   broker-salesperson
    d.   broker

96.   D. The fact that the hot water heater is not working is a material fact and must be disclosed. The other items may "stigmatize" the property but are not considered material facts.

97.   B. NRS 645.300.

98.   C. The duty of confidentiality lasts for one year after termination of the agency.

99.   B. Regulations are adopted by the Commissioners.

100.   D. Broker applicants must have two years of real estate experience in the last four years.

70639920R00026